KT-370-327

TAGINES
& COUSCOUS

RYLAND
PETERS
& SMALL
LONDON NEW YORK

TAGINES
& COUSCOUS

Delicious recipes for Moroccan one-pot cooking

Ghillie Başan

photography by Martin Brigdale and Peter Cassidy

Design and Photographic Art Direction Steve Painter
and Liz Sephton
Senior Commissioning Editor Julia Charles
Production Controller Toby Marshall
Art Director Leslie Harrington
Publishing Director Alison Starling

Photography Martin Brigdale and Peter Cassidy
Food Stylists Ross Dobson, Bridget Sargeson
and Lucy McKelvie
Prop Styling Martin Brigdale, Helen Trent
and Steve Painter
Indexer Hilary Bird

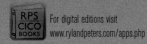

For digital editions visit
www.rylandpeters.com/apps.php

First published in the United Kingdom in 2010
by Ryland Peters & Small
20-21 Jockey's Fields
London WC1R 4BW
www.rylandpeters.com

10 9 8 7 6 5 4

Text © Ghillie Basan 2007, 2008, 2010
Design and commissioned photographs
© Ryland Peters & Small 2007, 2008, 2010
Printed in China

The author's moral rights have been asserted.
All rights reserved. No part of this publication
may be reproduced, stored in a retrieval system,
or transmitted in any form or by any means,
electronic, mechanical, photocopying, or otherwise,
without the prior permission of the publisher.

ISBN: 978 1 84597 947 8

A CIP record for this book is available from the
British Library.

Some of the recipes in this book have been
published previously by Ryland Peters & Small
in *Tagine* and *Flavours of Morocco*.

Notes
• All spoon measurements are level.
• All eggs are medium, unless otherwise specified.
Uncooked or partially cooked eggs should not be
served to the very young, the elderly, those with
a compromised immune system or pregnant women.
• When a recipe calls for the grated zest of citrus
fruit, buy unwaxed fruit and wash well before using.
If you can only find treated fruit, scrub well in warm
soapy water and rinse before using.
• Sterilize preserving jars before use. Wash in hot
soapy water and rinse in boiling water. Place in a
large saucepan, cover with hot water, bring to the
boil and boil, covered, for 15 minutes. Turn off the
heat and leave in the hot water until using. Invert
onto kitchen towel to dry. Sterilize lids for 5 minutes,
by boiling. Jars should be filled while hot.
• Ovens should be preheated to the specified
temperature. Recipes in this book were tested in
a regular oven. If using a fan-assisted oven, follow
the maker's instructions for adjusting temperatures.

Photography credits
© Martin Brigdale: Pages 4, 5, 132, 133
© Ryland Peters & Small by Martin Brigdale:
Pages 1 above, 2, 3, 14 below right, 16, 18, 21, 27,
30–35, 40, 43, 46–53, 56–60, 64–68, 72 below
left, 75, 78, 82, 86–93, 96–103, 114, 119, 120,
139, 141.
© Ryland Peters & Small by Peter Cassidy:
Pages 1 below, 6, 9–13, 14 above, below left &
below centre, 17, 22–24, 28, 36, 38, 39, 44, 45, 54,
55, 63, 70, 71, 72 above & below right, 77, 81, 84,
85, 94, 95, 104–113, 117, 118, 122–130, 135–138,
142, endpapers.

CONTENTS

the secrets of tagines

Colourful, decorative, scented and a feast for the senses – the food of Morocco reflects a fascinating mix of the cultures that have left their mark on the region: the indigenous Berbers with their tradition of tagine cooking and couscous; the nomadic Bedouins from the desert who brought dates, milk and grains; the Moors expelled from Spain who relied heavily on olives and olive oil and brought with them the Andalusian flavours of paprika and herbs; the Sephardic Jews with their preserving techniques employing salt; the Arabs who introduced the sophisticated cuisine from the Middle East; the Ottoman influence of kebabs and pastry making; and finally, the finesse of the French.

The root of Moroccan cooking can be traced back to the indigenous Berber tribes. Steeped in tradition, the rural Berbers are proud of their ancestry. They have lived in North Africa, between Egypt and the western coast of Morocco, as far back as archaeological records go. Originally farmers, living alongside the nomadic Taureg and Bedouin tribes of the desert, the Berbers have made an impact on the food of the region long before the invasion of the Arabs and, although they had to convert from Christianity to Islam and adopt new religious and culinary customs, they are keen to make the point that they are not of Arab descent. Many rural Berber communities speak their own languages and dialects but those who are literate also speak Arabic and, in some areas, French. Berbers also fiercely uphold some of their own culinary customs, such as the festive pilgrimages, moussems, which are held in tented enclosures where traditional dishes, such as

couscous, are cooked in vast quantities and shared. Another feature of Berber culinary life is the diffa, which is a festive banquet, varying in content in accordance with the wealth of the family, to mark special family occasions such as weddings and births and religious events.

It is Berbers we have to thank for tagines and couscous. A tagine is a glorified stew worthy of poetry – aromatic and syrupy, zesty and spicy, or sweet and fragrant are just some of the words that come to mind. It is a dish of tender meat, fish or succulent vegetables, simmered to perfection in buttery sauces with fruit, herbs, honey and chillies. An authentic tagine is in a class of its own and has become a fundamental feature of Moroccan cuisine.

The name 'tagine' (sometimes spelled 'tajine') is also given to the vessel in which the food is cooked: a shallow, round, earthenware pot with a unique conical lid designed to lock in moisture and flavours. In it, the food cooks gently in a small amount of liquid. The finished dish can either be served piping hot straight from its cooking vessel, or tipped into one of the decorative versions of the pot, glazed in beautiful shades of blue and green, to take to the table.

Although originally a Berber dish, the tagine has evolved with the history of the region as waves of Arab and Ottoman invaders, Moorish refugees from Andalusia and French colonialists have left their influences on the cuisine. Classic tagines include combinations of lamb with dried prunes or apricots; chicken with preserved lemon and green olives;

duck with dates and honey; and fish cooked with tomatoes, lime and fresh coriander. In the modern Maghreb, the Berbers are still renowned for their tasty, pungent tagines made with lots of onions and *smen*, a rancid clarified butter (see page 11) which is very much an acquired taste! The method employed in tagine cooking also varies from the countryside to the cities. In the north, in cities like Tangier and Casablanca, where the Spanish and French influences are evident, the meat is often browned in butter or oil and the spices and onions are sautéed before adding the rest of the ingredients, whereas Fassi and Marrakchi tagines are often prepared by putting all the ingredients together in water and then adding extra butter or *smen* towards the end of the cooking time.

Traditionally, tagines are served as a course on their own, with freshly baked flat breads or crusty bread to mop up the delectable syrupy sauces, and are followed by a mound of couscous. The more modern way is to combine the courses and serve them with an accompanying salad or vegetable side dish. On festive occasions, the custom is to pile up a huge pyramid of couscous and hollow out the peak to form a well into which the tagine is spooned. However, most earthenware tagines are not big enough to cope with feasts, so large copper pots are often used instead.

The great secret of an authentic tagine is to simmer the ingredients over a low heat, so that everything remains deliciously moist and tender. Meat tagines may be cooked for several hours, the meat simmering gently in a seasoned, fragrant liquid until it is so tender it almost falls off the bone. Generally, dishes of vegetables, pulses or fish do not require long cooking times but still benefit from the tagine method in terms of enhanced taste and texture. Traditionally, tagines are cooked over a clay stove, or brazier, which is stoked with charcoal to maintain constant heat. Such stoves diffuse the heat around the base of the tagine, enabling the liquid to reduce and thicken without drying out. Wood-burning ovens and open fires are used, too. However, wonderful tagines can also be produced using a modern hob or oven. Most authentic tagines have a little hole at the top of the conical lid to release some of the steam, so that it doesn't try to escape at the seam between the base and the lid. If there is no hole, you will probably need at intervals to tilt the lid at an angle to release the steam yourself. When cooking in an oven, it is generally only the base of the tagine that is used.

When it comes to buying a tagine, there are several different types and sizes, as some represent a Berber tribe, a particular village or a region of Morocco. There are a number of cooking tagines to choose from, but few of them come with a warning about their vulnerability over a conventional gas or electric hob. Most of the factory-made vessels, whether they are glazed or not, tend to form hairline cracks when they are placed over a gas flame; and they cannot be used on an electric ring. So what do you do? For a glazed earthenware tagine, a heat diffuser is essential, otherwise it is worth splashing out on the durable cast-iron version with a glazed, earthenware lid produced by Le Creuset. Their version looks just like a beautifully authentic glazed tagine but the cast-iron base enables it to be used safely on gas or electric hobs. A solid, heavy-based casserole is a good substitute, as long as you keep the heat very low. But for a tasty, succulent meal, full of flavour and adventure, it is well worth attempting to cook with the genuine article.

smen (aged butter)

This pungent butter, used as the primary cooking fat in some tagines, is left to mature in earthenware pots for months, sometimes years! You can substitute it with ghee (clarified butter).

500 g unsalted butter, at room temperature

1 tablespoon sea salt

1 tablespoon dried oregano

Makes about 500 g

Soften the butter in a bowl. Boil 150 ml water in a saucepan with the salt and oregano to reduce it a little, then strain it directly onto the butter. Stir the butter with a wooden spoon to make sure it is well blended, then let cool.

Knead the butter with your hands to bind it, squeezing out any excess water. Drain well and spoon the butter into a hot, sterilized jar (see note on page 4). Seal the jar and store it in a cool, dry place for at least 6 weeks.

preserved lemons

Added to dishes as a refreshing, tangy ingredient or garnish, preserved lemons are essential to the cooking of tagines. You can buy jars of ready-preserved lemons in specialist shops and some supermarkets, but it is worth making your own.

10 organic, unwaxed lemons, preferably the small, thin-skinned Meyer variety

10 tablespoons sea salt

freshly squeezed juice of 3–4 lemons

Makes 1 large jar

Wash and dry the lemons and slice the ends off each one. Stand each lemon on one end and make two vertical cuts three-quarters of the way through them, as if cutting them into quarters but keeping the base intact. Stuff 1 tablespoon salt into each lemon and pack them into a large sterilized jar (see note on page 4). Seal the jar and store the lemons in a cool place for 3–4 days to soften the skins.

Press the lemons down into the jar, so they are even more tightly packed. Pour the lemon juice over the salted lemons, until they are completely covered. Seal the jar again and store it in a cool place for at least 1 month. Rinse the salt off the preserved lemons before using.

harissa paste

This fiery paste is popular throughout North Africa. It can be served as a condiment, or as a dip for warm crusty bread, and it can be stirred into tagines and couscous to impart its distinctive chilli taste. This recipe is for the basic paste, to which other ingredients such as fennel seeds, fresh coriander and mint can be added. Jars of ready-prepared harissa are available in some supermarkets and specialist delicatessens but it's easy to make your own.

chermoula

A distinctive Moroccan marinade, chermoula is often employed in fish dishes as the flavours of chilli, ground cumin and fresh coriander marry so well and complement the fish perfectly.

2 garlic cloves, chopped

1 teaspoon coarse sea salt

1–2 teaspoons cumin seeds, crushed or ground

1 fresh red chilli, deseeded and chopped

freshly squeezed juice of 1 lemon

2 tablespoons olive oil

a small bunch of coriander, roughly chopped and/or a small bunch of flat leaf parsley, chopped

Makes 1 small pot

To make the chermoula, use a mortar and pestle to pound the garlic and chilli with the salt to form a paste. Add the coriander and parsley leaves and pound to a coarse paste. Beat in the cumin and paprika and bind well with the olive oil and lemon juice (you can whizz all the ingredients together in an electric blender, if you prefer).

8 dried red chillies (Horn or New Mexico), deseeded

2–3 garlic cloves, finely chopped

½ teaspoon sea salt

1 teaspoon ground cumin

1 teaspoon ground coriander

4 tablespoons olive oil

Makes about 4 tablespoons

Put the chillies in a bowl and pour over enough warm water to cover them. Leave them to soak for 1 hour. Drain and squeeze out any excess water. Using a mortar and pestle, pound them to a paste with the garlic and salt (or whizz them in an electric mixer). Beat in the cumin and coriander and bind with the olive oil.

Store the harissa in a sealed jar in the refrigerator with a thin layer of olive oil poured on top. It will keep well for about 1 month.

ras-el-hanout

There is no one recipe for *ras-el-hanout*, a lovely pungent spice mix, packed with strong Indian aromas of cinnamon, cloves and ginger combined with local African roots and the delicate, perfumed notes of rosebuds. Every family has its own favourite blend. Some of the spices are available only in the Maghreb, so if your tagine recipe calls for this flavouring your easiest solution is to select one of the ready-prepared spice mixes available in Middle Eastern and African stores – you can order a moist, aromatic ras-al-hanout online from spice specialists Seasoned Pioneers at www.seasonedpioneers.co.uk. Alternatively, you could try this version.

* *

1 teaspoon black peppercorns

1 teaspoon cloves

1 teaspoon aniseeds

1 teaspoon nigella seeds

1 teaspoon allspice berries

1 teaspoon cardamom seeds

2 teaspoons ground ginger

2 teaspoons ground turmeric

2 teaspoons coriander seeds

2 pieces mace

2 pieces cinnamon bark

2 teaspoons dried mint

1 dried red chilli

1 teaspoon dried lavender

6 dried rosebuds, broken up

Makes about 4–5 tablespoons

Using a mortar and pestle, or an electric blender, grind together all the spices to form a coarse powder.

Stir in the lavender and rose petals and tip the mixture into an airtight container.

You can store this spice mix for up to 6 months if you keep it in a cool cupboard and well away from direct sunlight.

traditional lamb tagines

lamb tagine with prunes, apricots and honey

A classic lamb tagine, sweetened with honey and fruit, is the perfect introduction to the tastes of Morocco. Traditionally, this aromatic dish is served with bread to mop up the syrupy sauce. To balance the sweetness, you could also serve a crunchy salad of finely shredded carrot, onions and cabbage or peppers, spiked with chilli.

• •

1–2 tablespoons ghee, or 1 tablespoon olive oil plus a knob of butter

2 tablespoons blanched almonds

2 red onions, finely chopped

2–3 garlic cloves, finely chopped

a thumb-sized piece of fresh ginger, peeled and chopped

a pinch of saffron threads

2 cinnamon sticks

1–2 teaspoons coriander seeds, crushed

500 g boned lamb, from the shoulder, leg or shanks, trimmed and cubed

12 dried, stoned prunes, soaked for 1 hour and drained

6 dried, stoned apricots, soaked for 1 hour and drained

3–4 strips orange zest

1–2 tablespoons dark, runny honey

leaves from a small bunch of fresh coriander leaves, finely chopped

sea salt and freshly ground black pepper

crusty bread, to serve

Serves 4–6

Heat the ghee in a tagine or heavy-based casserole, stir in the almonds and cook until they turn golden. Add the onions and garlic and sauté until they begin to colour. Stir in the ginger, saffron, cinnamon sticks and coriander seeds. Toss in the lamb, making sure it is coated in the onion and spices, and sauté for 1–2 minutes.

Pour in enough water to just cover the meat and bring it to the boil. Reduce the heat, cover the tagine or casserole and simmer for about 1 hour, until the meat is tender. Add the prunes, apricots and orange zest, cover the tagine again, and simmer for a further 15–20 minutes. Stir in the honey, season with salt and pepper to taste, cover and simmer for a further 10 minutes. Make sure there is enough liquid in the pot, as you want the sauce to be syrupy and slightly caramelized, but not too dry – add a little more water if necessary.

Stir in some of the coriander and reserve the rest to sprinkle over the top of the dish. Serve immediately with crusty bread.

lamb tagine with dates, almonds and pistachios

In Arab culture, dates are an age-old source of nutrition and natural sugar; nomads could survive in the desert with dates alone for nourishment. As the fruit is regarded as special, it is often added to festive grain dishes and stews. This slightly sticky date and nut tagine is a favourite at weddings and other family feasts.

◆ ◆

2–3 tablespoons ghee, or 1 tablespoon olive oil plus a knob of butter

2 onions, finely chopped

1–2 teaspoons ground turmeric

1 teaspoon ground ginger

2 teaspoons ground cinnamon

1 kg lean lamb, from the shoulder, neck or leg, cut into bite-sized pieces

250 g ready-to-eat stoned dates

1 tablespoon dark, runny honey

1 tablespoon olive oil

a knob of butter

2–3 tablespoons blanched almonds

2 tablespoons shelled pistachios

leaves from a small bunch of fresh flat leaf parsley, finely chopped

sea salt and freshly ground black pepper

Plain, Buttery Couscous (see page 108), to serve

Serves 4

Heat the ghee in a tagine or heavy-based casserole. Stir in the onions and sauté until golden brown. Stir in the turmeric, ginger and cinnamon. Toss in the meat, making sure it is coated in the spice mixture. Pour in enough water to almost cover the meat and bring it to the boil. Reduce the heat, cover with a lid and simmer gently for roughly 1½ hours.

Add the dates and stir in the honey. Cover with a lid again and simmer for another 30 minutes. Season with salt and lots of black pepper.

Heat the olive oil with the butter in a small pan. Stir in the almonds and pistachios and cook until they begin to turn golden brown.

Scatter the toasted nuts over the lamb and dates and sprinkle with the flat leaf parsley. Serve with Plain, Buttery Couscous and a sharp, crunchy salad with preserved lemon to cut the sweetness.

lamb tagine with shallots and dates

Commonly known as the 'bread of the desert' the Arabs and the Berbers treat dates as a sacred food source as they and their ancestors have survived off them for generations, even when there has been little else to eat. They also symbolize hospitality and prosperity, so they are offered to guests and they are popped into numerous tagines and couscous dishes.

* *

3 tablespoons ghee, or 2 tablespoons olive oil plus a knob of butter

700 g lean boned lamb, from the shoulder or neck, trimmed and cut into bite-sized pieces

12 shallots, peeled and left whole

4–6 garlic cloves, peeled and left whole

2 teaspoons ground turmeric

2 cinnamon sticks

1–2 tablespoons dark, runny honey

225 g ready-to-eat stoned dates

1–2 tablespoons sesame seeds, toasted

sea salt and freshly ground black pepper

crusty bread or Plain, Buttery Couscous (see page 108), to serve

Serves 4–6

Heat the ghee in a tagine or heavy-based casserole. Toss in the lamb and brown it all over. Using a slotted spoon, remove the meat from the tagine and set aside. Add the shallots and garlic and sauté, stirring occasionally, until they begin to colour.

Add the turmeric and cinnamon sticks and return the meat to the tagine. Pour in just enough water to cover the meat then bring it to the boil. Reduce the heat, cover with the lid and simmer for about 1 hour, giving it a stir from time to time.

Stir in the honey and season with salt and plenty of black pepper. Add the dates, replace the lid, and cook for a further 25–30 minutes.

Sprinkle with the toasted sesame seeds and serve with crusty bread or Plain, Buttery Couscous.

baked lamb tagine with quinces, figs and honey

In this festive dish, a shoulder of lamb is marinated in chermoula – a delicious Moroccan herb and spice mix – and baked slowly. If you have difficulty sourcing quinces, you can use sharp green apples or pears instead.

• •

1.5 kg shoulder of lamb on the bone

1 quantity of Chermoula (see page 12)

2 tablespoons ghee, or 1 tablespoon olive oil plus a knob of butter

2 red onions, cut into wedges

225 g ready-to-eat prunes, stoned

225 g ready-to-eat dried figs, or fresh figs, halved

40 g butter

2 fresh quinces, quartered and cored (keep soaked in water with a squeeze of lemon until ready to use)

2–3 tablespoons orange flower water

2 tablespoons dark, runny honey

leaves from a small bunch of fresh flat leaf parsley, chopped

leaves from a small bunch of fresh coriander, chopped

Plain, Buttery Couscous (see page 108) or roasted potatoes, to serve

Serves 4–6

Cut small incisions in the shoulder of lamb with a sharp knife and rub the chermoula well into the meat. Cover and leave in the refrigerator for at least 6 hours, or overnight.

Preheat the oven to 180°C (350°F) Gas 4.

Heat the ghee in a tagine or heavy-based casserole, add the lamb and brown it all over. Transfer the meat to a plate. Stir the onions and any leftover chermoula into the ghee. Add the prunes and if using dried figs add them at this stage. Pour in 300 ml water and put the lamb back into the tagine. Cover with the lid and put the tagine in the oven for about 2 hours.

Towards the end of the cooking time, melt the butter in a heavy-based pan, toss in the quinces and sauté until golden brown. Remove the tagine from the oven and place the golden quince around the meat (if using fresh figs, add them at this stage). Splash the orange flower water over the lamb and drizzle the honey over the meat and the fruit. Return the tagine to the oven for a further 25–30 minutes, until the meat and fruit are nicely browned and the lamb is so tender it almost falls off the bone.

Sprinkle the chopped parsley and coriander over the top and serve immediately with Plain, Buttery Couscous or roasted potatoes.

lamb tagine with chestnuts, saffron and pomegranate seeds

This is a lovely winter dish, decorated with jewel-like ruby-red pomegranate seeds. Whole, meaty chestnuts are often used in Arab-influenced culinary cultures as a substitute for potatoes. You can use freshly roasted nuts or ready-peeled, vacuum-packed or frozen chestnuts.

• •

2 tablespoons ghee, or 1 tablespoon olive oil plus a knob of butter

2 onions, finely chopped

4 garlic cloves, finely chopped

thumb-sized piece of fresh ginger, peeled and finely chopped or shredded

a pinch of saffron threads

1–2 cinnamon sticks

1 kg lean lamb, from the shoulder or leg, cut into bite-sized pieces

250 g peeled chestnuts

1–2 tablespoons dark, runny honey

seeds of 1 pomegranate, pith removed

leaves from a small bunch of fresh mint, chopped

leaves from a small bunch of fresh coriander, chopped

sea salt and freshly ground black pepper

crusty bread or Plain, Buttery Couscous (see page 108), to serve

Serves 4

Heat the ghee in a tagine or heavy-based casserole. Stir in the onions, garlic and ginger and sauté until they begin to colour. Add the saffron and cinnamon sticks, and toss in the lamb. Pour in enough water to almost cover the meat and bring it to the boil. Reduce the heat, cover with a lid and simmer gently for about 1 hour.

Add the chestnuts and stir in the honey. Cover with the lid again and cook gently for a further 30 minutes, until the meat is very tender.

Season to taste with salt and plenty of black pepper and then toss in some of the pomegranate seeds, mint and coriander. Sprinkle the remaining pomegranate seeds and herbs over the lamb, and serve with crusty bread or Plain, Buttery Couscous.

See photograph on page 31.

tfaia tagine with onions, browned almonds and eggs

Originally from Andalusia, tfaia tagines are popular in northern Morocco, particularly in Tangier. Their trademark is a pungent, nutty flavour that emanates from matured, clarified butter called *smen* which is an acquired taste for some people. The recipe works just as well with ghee, which is ordinary clarified butter.

* *

1–2 tablespoons ghee or smen
(see page 11)

2 garlic cloves, crushed

1 teaspoon ground ginger

1 teaspoon ground coriander

1 teaspoon saffron threads, ground
with a pinch of salt

1 kg lamb cutlets

2 onions, finely chopped

175 g black Kalamata olives, stoned

2 preserved lemons (see page 11),
cut into quarters

leaves from a small bunch of fresh
coriander, chopped

sea salt and freshly ground
black pepper

To serve:

4 eggs

½ teaspoon ground saffron, or
a pinch of saffron threads

½ tablespoon ghee or butter

2 tablespoons blanched almonds

crusty bread

Serves 4

Melt the ghee in a tagine or heavy-based casserole. Stir in the garlic, ginger, ground coriander and saffron, and roll the lamb cutlets in the mixture. Sprinkle the onions over the cutlets and pour in just enough water to cover the meat. Bring the water to the boil, reduce the heat, cover with a lid and cook gently for about 1½ hours.

Add the olives and lemons and cook, uncovered, for about another 20 minutes to reduce the sauce. Season well with plenty of salt and black pepper and toss in the chopped coriander.

Meanwhile, boil the eggs in their shells for about 4 minutes, so that the yolk is just firm, and shell them. Dissolve the saffron in 2 tablespoons warm water and roll the eggs in the yellow liquid to colour them. Cut the eggs in half lengthways.

In a frying pan, melt the ghee and stir in the almonds until golden brown. Sprinkle the toasted almonds over the tagine and arrange the eggs around the edge. Serve immediately with crusty bread.

summer tagine of lamb, courgettes, peppers and mint

Summer tagines using seasonal vegetables are often quite light and colourful. Other vegetables that might be added to this tagine include tomatoes, aubergines and peas. This dish is particularly good served with wedges of lemon to squeeze over it, or with finely shredded preserved lemon sprinkled over the top.

• •

3–4 tablespoons olive oil

1 onion, roughly chopped

4 garlic cloves, roughly chopped

1 teaspoon cumin seeds

1 teaspoon coriander seeds

1 teaspoon dried mint

thumb-sized piece of fresh ginger, peeled and finely chopped or grated

750 g lean lamb, from the shoulder or leg, cut into bite-sized pieces

2 small courgettes, sliced thickly on the diagonal

1 red or yellow pepper, deseeded and cut into thick strips

4 tomatoes, skinned, deseeded and cut into chunks

leaves from a small bunch of fresh flat leaf parsley, roughly chopped

leaves from a small bunch of fresh mint, roughly chopped

sea salt and freshly ground black pepper

1 lemon, cut into quarters, to serve

Serves 4–6

Heat the olive oil in a tagine or heavy-based casserole. Stir in the onion, garlic, cumin and coriander seeds, dried mint and ginger. Once the onions begin to soften, toss in the meat and pour in enough water to just cover it. Bring the water to the boil, reduce the heat, cover with a lid and cook gently for about 1½ hours.

Season the cooking juices with salt and pepper. Add the courgettes, pepper and tomatoes, tucking them around the meat (add a little more water if necessary). Cover with a lid again and cook for about 15 minutes, until the courgettes and pepper are cooked but retain a bite.

Toss in some of the chopped parsley and mint, sprinkle the rest over the top and serve immediately with lemon wedges on the side to squeeze over the dish.

lamb k'dra with sweet potatoes and okra

This is a Berber dish which is often prepared with large cuts of meat, such as shanks, knuckle or sheeps' heads, which are removed at the end of the cooking and arranged around a mound of couscous. The vegetables are arranged on top and the cooking broth is served separately to spoon over the dish.

* *

6–8 lamb shanks, trimmed and cut
into bite-sized pieces

6 onions, halved lengthways and
sliced crossways

a pinch of saffron threads

2 cinnamon sticks

1 teaspoon ground black pepper

2 sweet potatoes, peeled, halved
lengthways and thickly sliced

2 tablespoons ghee, smen
(see page 11) or butter

250 g fresh okra

freshly squeezed juice of 1 lemon

sea salt

crusty bread or Plain, Buttery
Couscous (see page 108), to serve

Serves 6–8

Put the lamb in a tagine or large heavy-based casserole with half of the onions, saffron, cinnamon sticks and black pepper. Pour in enough water to cover the meat and bring it to the boil. Reduce the heat, cover with a lid and simmer gently for about 1½ hours (top up with water if necessary).

Add the sweet potatoes, the ghee and the rest of the onions. Simmer for a further 20–25 minutes, until the potatoes are tender. Meanwhile, toss the okra in the lemon juice, leave for 10 minutes, then drain. Add the okra to the casserole and simmer for a further 5–10 minutes, until the okra is cooked through but still retains a crunch.

Season to taste with salt and serve with crusty bread or Plain, Buttery Couscous.

beef, kefta and sausage tagines

beef tagine with beetroot and oranges

Earthy and fruity, with a hint of ginger, this tagine is a good winter warmer. It can be made with either fresh or pre-cooked beetroot. You could serve it with roasted butternut squash and a mound of Plain, Buttery Couscous tossed with pistachios.

• •

1–2 tablespoons ghee, or 1 tablespoon olive oil plus a knob of butter

3–4 garlic cloves, crushed

1 red onion, halved lengthways and sliced with the grain

40 g fresh ginger, peeled and finely chopped or grated

1 red chilli, deseeded and sliced

2 teaspoons coriander seeds, crushed

2 cinnamon sticks

3–4 beetroots, peeled and quartered

500 g lean beef, cut into bite-sized cubes or strips

2 thin-skinned oranges, cut into segments

1 tablespoon dark, runny honey

1–2 tablespoons orange flower water

a knob of butter

2–3 tablespoons shelled pistachios

leaves from a small bunch of fresh flat leaf parsley, roughly chopped

sea salt and freshly ground black pepper

Plain, Buttery Couscous (see page 108), to serve

Serves 4–6

Melt the ghee in a tagine or heavy-based casserole, add the garlic, onion and ginger and stir until they begin to colour. Add the chilli, coriander seeds and cinnamon sticks. Add the beetroot and sauté for 2–3 minutes. Toss in the beef and sauté for 1 minute. Pour in enough water to almost cover the beef and beetroot and bring to the boil. Reduce the heat, cover with a lid and simmer for 1 hour, until the meat is very tender.

Add the orange segments, honey and orange flower water to the tagine and season to taste with salt and pepper. Cover with the lid and cook for a further 10–15 minutes.

Melt the butter in a small saucepan and toss in the pistachios, stirring them over medium heat until they turn golden brown. Sprinkle them over the tagine along with the flat leaf parsley and serve immediately.

beef tagine with sweet potatoes, peas, ginger and ras-el-hanout

This fairly fiery dish is laced with the powerful flavours and aromas of ras-el-hanout, a traditional spice mix. Regional variations use turnip, yam, pumpkin or butternut squash instead of sweet potatoes. It is best served with chunks of crusty bread and cooling yoghurt or a glass of mint tea.

* *

2 tablespoons ghee or smen
(see page 11), or 1 tablespoon olive oil
plus a knob of butter

40 g fresh ginger, peeled and
finely shredded

1 onion, finely chopped

1 kg lean beef, cut into bite-sized
pieces

1–2 teaspoons ras-el-hanout
(see page 15)

2 sweet potatoes, peeled and cubed

500 g fresh or frozen peas

2–3 tomatoes, skinned, deseeded
and chopped

1 preserved lemon (see page 11),
finely shredded or chopped

leaves from a small bunch of fresh
coriander, finely chopped

sea salt and freshly ground
black pepper

crusty bread and natural yoghurt,
to serve

Serves 4

Heat the ghee in a tagine or heavy-based casserole. Add in the ginger and onion and sauté until soft. Toss in the beef and sear it on all sides, then stir in the ras-el-hanout. Pour in enough water to just cover the meat and bring it to the boil. Reduce the heat, cover with the lid and cook gently for about 40 minutes.

Add the sweet potato to the tagine, season to taste with salt and pepper, cover with the lid and cook gently for a further 20 minutes, until the meat is tender. Toss in the peas and tomatoes, cover with the lid and cook for 5–10 minutes.

Sprinkle the preserved lemon and chopped coriander over the top and serve immediately with crusty bread and natural yoghurt.

kefta tagine with eggs and roasted cumin

Variations of this great street dish can be found throughout the Maghreb. It is also often prepared as a snack in the home. In many households, kefta (poached meatballs) are prepared in batches and stored in the refrigerator. Kefta are usually quite fiery, so serve them with plenty of good bread and natural yoghurt to temper their hotness.

* *

For the kefta:

225 g finely minced lamb

1 onion, finely chopped

1 teaspoon dried mint

*1–2 teaspoons ras-el-hanout
(see page 15)*

½ teaspoon cayenne pepper

*leaves from a small bunch of fresh
flat leaf parsley, finely chopped*

*sea salt and freshly ground
black pepper*

1 tablespoon butter

¼–½ teaspoon salt

*1 teaspoon cayenne pepper or
½ teaspoon dried chilli flakes*

4 eggs

*1–2 teaspoons cumin seeds,
dry-roasted and ground*

*leaves from a small bunch of fresh
flat leaf parsley, roughly chopped*

*crusty bread and natural yoghurt,
to serve*

Serves 4

To make the kefta, put the minced lamb, onion, mint, ras-el-hanout, cayenne pepper and parsley in a bowl. Season to taste with salt and pepper and mix well together. Using your hands, knead the mixture and mould it into small walnut-sized balls, so that you end up with about 12 balls.

Fill a tagine or heavy-casserole with water and bring it to the boil. Carefully drop in the kefta, a few at a time, and poach them for about 10 minutes, turning them so that they are cooked on all sides. Remove them with a slotted spoon and drain on kitchen paper. Reserve roughly 300 ml of the cooking liquid. (If not using the kefta immediately, transfer them to a plate to cool and store covered in the refrigerator for 2–3 days.)

Add the butter to the reserved cooking liquid in the tagine and bring the mixture to the boil. Stir in the salt and cayenne pepper and drop in the poached kefta. Cook over high heat until almost all the liquid has evaporated. Carefully crack the eggs around the kefta, cover with a lid and leave the eggs to cook in the sauce and steam until they are just set.

Sprinkle the roasted cumin and chopped parsley over the top of the dish and serve immediately with crusty bread and natural yoghurt.

spicy kefta tagine with lemon

Kefta tagines don't require long cooking times as generally the sauce is made first and the meatballs are poached in it. This popular recipe is light and lemony and delicious served with Plain, Buttery Couscous tossed with chilli and herbs and a leafy salad.

◆ ◆

For the kefta:

450 g finely minced beef or lamb

1 onion, finely chopped or grated

leaves from a small bunch of fresh flat leaf parsley, finely chopped

1–2 teaspoons ground cinnamon

1 teaspoon ground cumin

1 teaspoon ground coriander

½ teaspoon cayenne pepper

sea salt and freshly ground black pepper

1 tablespoon each olive oil and butter

1 onion, roughly chopped

2–3 garlic cloves, halved and crushed

a thumb-sized piece of fresh ginger, peeled and finely chopped

1 red chilli, thinly sliced

2 teaspoons ground turmeric

leaves from a small bunch of fresh coriander, chopped

leaves from a small bunch of fresh mint, chopped

freshly squeezed juice of 1 lemon

1 lemon, cut into wedges, pips removed

Plain, Buttery Couscous (see page 108), tossed with finely chopped red chilli and fresh green herbs

Serves 4–6

To make the kefta, pound the minced meat with your knuckles in a bowl. Using your hands, lift up the lump of minced meat and slap it back down into the bowl. Add the onion, parsley, cinnamon, cumin, coriander and cayenne, and season to taste with salt and black pepper. Using your hands, mix the ingredients together and knead well, pounding the mixture for a few minutes. Take pieces of the mixture and shape them into little walnut-sized balls, so that you end up with about 16 kefta. (These can be made ahead of time and kept in the refrigerator for 2–3 days.)

Heat the oil and butter in a tagine or heavy-based casserole. Stir in the onion, garlic, ginger and chilli and sauté until they begin to brown. Add the turmeric and half the coriander and mint, and pour in 300 ml water. Bring to the boil, reduce the heat and simmer, covered, for 10 minutes. Carefully place the kefta in the liquid, cover and poach for about 15 minutes, rolling them in the liquid from time to time so they are cooked well on all sides. Pour over the lemon juice, season the liquid with salt and tuck the lemon segments around the kefta. Poach for a further 10 minutes.

Sprinkle with the remaining coriander and mint and serve with Plain, Buttery Couscous tossed with chilli and herbs and a leafy salad, if liked.

chickpea and chorizo tagine with bay leaves, paprika and sage

This is a classic, Spanish-influenced peasant dish, which is often eaten on its own with yoghurt and bread, but is also served with grilled or roasted meats, such as lamb chops. Either chorizo or Moroccan merguez sausages can be used, as both impart their spicy flavours to the dish. For a meatless version, just omit the sausage, as the chickpeas are extremely tasty on their own.

• •

175 g dried chickpeas, soaked overnight in plenty of water

2–3 tablespoons olive oil

2 red onions, cut in half lengthways, halved crossways, and sliced with the grain

2 garlic cloves, chopped

1 thin chorizo, roughly 15 cm long, sliced on the diagonal, or 450 g merguez sausages

2–3 fresh bay leaves

several sprigs of fresh thyme

1–2 teaspoons Spanish smoked paprika (pimentòn)

leaves from a small bunch of fresh sage, shredded

freshly squeezed juice of 1 lemon

sea salt and freshly ground black pepper

warmed flat breads and natural yoghurt, to serve

Serves 4

Drain the chickpeas, put them in a large saucepan and cover with plenty of water. Bring the water to the boil, reduce the heat and simmer for roughly 45 minutes or until the chickpeas are soft but still have a bite to them. Drain well and refresh under cold running water. Remove any loose skins and discard them.

Heat the olive oil in a tagine or heavy-based casserole. Stir in the onions and garlic and sauté until they begin to colour. Add the chorizo, bay leaves and thyme and sauté until lightly browned. Toss in the chickpeas, add the paprika and cover with a lid. Cook gently for 10–15 minutes, to allow the flavours to mingle.

Add in the sage leaves and lemon juice and gently toss. Season to taste with salt and pepper and serve hot with warmed flat breads and natural yoghurt.

chorizo tagine with lentils and fenugreek

This is very simple yet delicious peasant food. Prepared with locally-cured, spicy Moroccan merguez sausages or chorizo and lentils or beans, it is a satisfying dish, best served with flat breads and a generous dollop of creamy yoghurt.

* *

2 tablespoons olive oil

2 onions, chopped

2 garlic cloves, chopped

450 g chorizo or merguez sausage, thickly sliced

2 teaspoons ground turmeric

2 teaspoons ground fenugreek

225 g brown lentils

400-g tin chopped tomatoes

2 teaspoons sugar

leaves from a bunch of fresh coriander, roughly chopped (reserve some to garnish)

sea salt and freshly ground black pepper

warmed flat breads and natural yoghurt, to serve

Serves 4–6

Heat the oil in a tagine or heavy-based casserole. Add the onions and garlic and sauté until they begin to colour. Toss in the chorizo slices and sauté for 1–2 minutes just to flavour the oil. Stir in the turmeric and fenugreek and add the lentils, making sure they are well coated with the spices.

Add the tomatoes with the sugar and pour in enough water to cover the lentils by 2.5 cm. Bring the liquid to the boil, reduce the heat, put on the lid and cook gently for about 25 minutes, adding more water if necessary, until the lentils are tender but not mushy.

Toss in the coriander and season to taste with salt and pepper. Scatter the rest of the coriander over the top and serve with warmed flat breads and natural yoghurt.

chicken and duck tagines

chicken tagine with preserved lemon, green olives and thyme

Preserved lemon and cracked green olives are two of the principal ingredients of traditional Moroccan cooking. You can buy the olives at Middle Eastern and North African stores and some delicatessens. The tagine can be made with chicken joints or a whole chicken. Serve with Plain, Buttery couscous and a leafy salad or steamed carrots tossed with fresh mint.

* *

8–10 chicken thighs or 4 whole legs

2 tablespoons ghee or 1 tablespoon olive oil plus a knob of butter

2 preserved lemons (see page 11), cut into strips

175 g cracked green olives

1–2 teaspoons dried thyme or oregano

Plain, Buttery Couscous (see page 108), to serve

For the marinade:

1 onion, grated

3 garlic cloves, crushed

25 g fresh ginger, peeled and grated

leaves from a small bunch of fresh coriander, finely chopped

a pinch of saffron threads

freshly squeezed juice of 1 lemon

1 teaspoon coarse sea salt

3–4 tablespoons olive oil

sea salt and freshly ground black pepper

Serves 4

First make the marinade. Mix together all the ingredients together in a small bowl. Put the chicken thighs or legs in a shallow dish and coat them in the marinade, rubbing it into the skin. Cover and chill in the refrigerator for 1–2 hours.

Heat the olive oil with the butter in a tagine or heavy-based casserole. Remove the chicken pieces from the marinade and brown them in the oil. Pour over the marinade that is left in the dish and add enough water to come halfway up the sides of the chicken pieces. Bring the water to the boil, reduce the heat, cover and simmer for about 45 minutes, turning the chicken from time to time.

Add the preserved lemon, olives and half the thyme to the tagine. Cover and simmer for a further 15–20 minutes. Season to taste with salt and pepper and sprinkle the remaining thyme over the top. Serve with Plain, Buttery Couscous and steamed carrots tossed with fresh mint, if liked.

chicken tagine with harissa, artichokes and green grapes

With the tangy notes of preserved lemon combined with the sweet grapes, this tagine is deliciously refreshing and is best accompanied by warmed flat breads. This recipe uses ready-prepared artichoke hearts which are available tinned or frozen.

· ·

4 chicken breasts, cut into thick strips or chunks

2 tablespoons olive oil

2 onions, halved lengthways and sliced with the grain

½ preserved lemon (see page 11), thinly sliced

1–2 teaspoons sugar

1–2 teaspoons harissa paste (see page 12)

2 teaspoons tomato purée

300 ml chicken stock or water

390-g tin artichoke hearts, drained, rinsed and halved

16 green grapes, halved lengthways

leaves from a bunch of fresh coriander, coarsely chopped

sea salt and freshly ground black pepper

warmed flat breads, to serve

For the marinade:

2 garlic cloves, crushed

1 teaspoon ground turmeric

freshly squeezed juice of 1 lemon

1 tablespoon olive oil

Serves 4

First, make the marinade. Mix all the ingredients together in a large bowl. Add the chicken breasts to the bowl and toss them in the mixture, then cover and leave in the refrigerator to marinate for 1–2 hours.

Heat the oil in a tagine or heavy-based casserole. Add the onions, preserved lemon and sugar and sauté for 2–3 minutes, until slightly caramelized. Toss in the marinated chicken, then add the harissa and tomato purée. Pour in the stock and bring it to the boil. Reduce the heat, cover and simmer gently for 15 minutes.

Add the artichoke hearts, cover and cook for a further 5 minutes. Add the grapes with some of the coriander and season to taste with salt and pepper. Sprinkle with the remaining coriander and serve with warmed flat breads and a leafy salad, if liked.

spicy chicken tagine with apricots, rosemary and ginger

This tagine is both fruity and spicy, and the rosemary and ginger give it a delightful aroma. It can also be made with chicken joints or pigeon breasts, pheasant or duck, and needs only Plain, Buttery Couscous and a leafy salad to accompany it.

• •

2 tablespoons olive oil plus a knob of butter

1 onion, finely chopped

3 fresh rosemary sprigs, 1 finely chopped, the other 2 cut in half

40 g fresh ginger, peeled and finely chopped

2 fresh red chillies, deseeded and finely chopped

1–2 cinnamon sticks

8 chicken thighs

175 g ready-to-eat dried apricots

2 tablespoons clear, runny honey

400-g tin plum tomatoes with juice

sea salt and freshly ground black pepper

leaves from a small bunch of fresh green or purple basil

Plain, Buttery Couscous (see page 108), to serve

Serves 4

Heat the oil and butter in a tagine or heavy-based casserole. Add the onion, chopped rosemary, ginger and chillies and sauté until the onion begins to soften.

Stir in the halved rosemary sprigs and the cinnamon sticks. Add the chicken thighs and brown them on both sides. Toss in the apricots with the honey, then stir in the plum tomatoes with their juice. (Add a little water if necessary, to ensure there is enough liquid to cover the base of the tagine and submerge the apricots.) Bring the liquid to the boil, then reduce the heat. Cover and simmer gently for 35–40 minutes, until the chicken is cooked through.

Season to taste with salt and pepper. Shred the larger basil leaves and leave the small ones intact. Sprinkle them over the chicken and serve with Plain, Buttery Couscous and a leafy salad, if liked.

chicken k'dra with chickpeas, raisins and red peppers

A Moroccan k'dra is a stew cooked in smen, the traditional fermented butter, in a large copper pot (a k'dra). The other feature of a k'dra is the large quantity of onions used in the dish. It is best served on its own with a little bread, and some wedges of lemon to squeeze over it.

• •

1 chicken, about 1.5 kg, jointed into 6 pieces

175 g dried chickpeas, soaked overnight in plenty of water and drained

6 onions, finely chopped

1–2 cinnamon sticks

2 pinches of saffron threads

1 teaspoon each of sea salt and freshly ground black pepper

2 red peppers

3–4 tablespoons olive oil

3–4 tablespoons raisins or sultanas

2 tablespoons ghee, smen (see page 11) or butter

leaves from a bunch of fresh flat leaf parsley, finely chopped

lemon wedges, to serve

crusty bread, to serve

Serves 4–6

Put the chicken in a large heavy-based casserole. Add the chickpeas, 2 tablespoons of the chopped onion, cinnamon sticks and saffron and season with salt and pepper. Pour in enough water to cover the chicken and chickpeas by about 2.5 cm and bring to the boil. Cover, reduce the heat and simmer gently for about 1 hour, checking the water level from time to time.

Meanwhile, preheat the oven to 180°C (350°F) Gas 4. Put the peppers in a baking dish and pour over the oil. Bake in the preheated oven for about 30 minutes, until tender and the skin has buckled slightly. Remove from the oven and leave until cool enough to handle. Peel the skin off the peppers, cut in half lengthways, remove the stalk and seeds and cut the flesh into strips. Set aside.

Check the chicken and chickpeas, both of which should be tender, and add the rest of the onions with the raisins, butter and half of the parsley. Cover and cook gently for a further 40 minutes, until the onions have almost formed a purée and there is very little liquid left in the casserole.

Arrange the chicken joints on a serving dish and spoon the chickpea mixture around them. Scatter the strips of pepper over the top and serve with lemon wedges and crusty bread or Plain, Buttery Couscous.

chicken k'dra with turnips and chickpeas

Traditionally cooked in a large copper pot, k'dra dishes are often packed with plenty of vegetables and pulses to create a hearty, filling dish for a big family or a large gathering of people.

* *

1 kg chicken thighs

1–2 tablespoons ground turmeric

2–3 tablespoons olive oil plus a knob of butter

2 onions, coarsely chopped

4 garlic cloves, chopped

2–3 teaspoons coriander seeds

225 g dried chickpeas, soaked overnight in plenty of water and drained

450 g turnip flesh, cut into bite-sized pieces, or 8 baby turnips, halved

1 tablespoon ghee, melted (optional)

leaves from a bunch of fresh flat leaf parsley, coarsely chopped

sea salt and freshly ground black pepper

crusty bread, to serve

Serves 4–6

Trim the chicken thighs and rub them with the ground turmeric. Set aside.

Heat the oil and butter in a large copper pot, or heavy-based saucepan. Add the onions, garlic and coriander seeds and stir until they begin to colour.

Add the chicken thighs and brown lightly, then toss in the chickpeas and cover with 850 ml water. Bring to the boil, reduce the heat, cover and simmer for about 45 minutes, until the chicken and chickpeas are tender.

Add the turnip and a little extra water if necessary and cook for a further 10–15 minutes, depending on the type of turnip, until cooked but still firm. Season to taste with salt and pepper, pour over the melted ghee, if using, and garnish with the chopped parsley. Serve with crusty bread.

tagine of duck breasts with dates, honey and orange flower water

This traditional Moorish dish appears in various guises throughout the Arab-influenced world. Poultry cooked with dates and honey is probably one of the most ancient culinary combinations and the finished dish is deliciously succulent. You can substitute the duck with chicken, pigeon or poussins, if you prefer.

* *

25 g fresh ginger, peeled and chopped

2–3 garlic cloves, chopped

2–3 tablespoons olive oil plus
a knob of butter

2 cinnamon sticks

4 duck breasts, on the bone

2–3 tablespoons clear, runny honey

225 g ready-to-eat stoned dates

1–2 tablespoons orange flower water

sea salt and freshly ground
black pepper

1 tablespoon butter

2–3 tablespoons blanched almonds

Plain, Buttery Couscous (see page 108) tossed with finely chopped preserved lemon (see page 11) and fresh green herbs, to serve

Serves 4

Using a mortar and pestle, pound the ginger and garlic to a paste. Heat the olive oil and butter in a tagine or heavy-based casserole, then stir in the ginger-garlic paste and the cinnamon sticks. Once the mixture begins to colour, add the duck breasts and brown the skin.

Stir in the honey and tuck the dates around the duck. Add enough water (the amount will vary according to the size of your tagine) to cover the base of the tagine and to come about one-third of the way up the duck breasts. Bring to the boil, reduce the heat and cover. Cook gently for about 25 minutes.

Add the orange flower water and season to taste with salt and pepper. Cover and cook for a further 5 minutes, or until the duck is tender.

In a frying pan, melt the butter and stir in the almonds. Sauté until golden brown and then scatter them over the duck. Serve immediately with Plain, Buttery Couscous flavoured with preserved lemon and herbs.

duck tagine with pears and cinnamon

This traditional tagine can be prepared with duck, chicken, poussin or quails. Variations of the recipe can include quince, plums, apples, cherries and apricots. Serve the tagine with bread to mop up the syrupy juices or with Plain, Buttery Couscous.

* *

*2 tablespoons olive oil plus
a knob of butter*

2 onions, finely chopped

*25 g fresh ginger, peeled and
finely chopped*

2 cinnamon sticks

a pinch of saffron threads

*1 kg duck meat, from the thigh,
breast or leg, off the bone and
cut into bite-sized pieces*

2 tablespoons butter

3–4 tablespoons clear, runny honey

3 pears, peeled, quartered and cored

2–3 tablespoons orange flower water

*sea salt and freshly ground
black pepper*

1–2 tablespoons toasted sesame seeds

*a few lemon balm leaves, to garnish
(optional)*

*crusty bread or Plain, Buttery
Couscous (see page 108), to serve*

Serves 4–6

Heat the oil and butter in a tagine or heavy-based saucepan. Add the onions and ginger and sauté until they begin to colour, then add the cinnamon sticks and saffron. Toss in the duck meat, making sure it is well coated in the ginger and onions. Pour in roughly 600 ml water and bring it to the boil. Reduce the heat, cover and simmer gently for about 40 minutes, until the duck is tender.

Meanwhile, melt the butter in a heavy-based saucepan and stir in the honey. Toss in the pears and cook gently until they begin to caramelize. Add the pears to the duck with the orange flower water and cook the tagine for a further 10 minutes.

Season to taste with salt and pepper and scatter the roasted sesame seeds over the top. Garnish with the lemon balm leaves, if using, and serve with crusty bread or Plain, Buttery Couscous.

fish and seafood tagines

fish tagine with preserved lemon and mint

The fish tagines of coastal Morocco are often made with whole fish, or with large chunks of fleshy fish such as sea bass, monkfish and cod. The fish is first marinated in a chermoula-style flavouring, and the dish is given an additional fillip with a little white wine or sherry. Serve with new potatoes and a leafy salad.

• •

900 g fresh fish fillets, such as cod or haddock, cut into large chunks

2–3 tablespoons olive oil

1 red onion, finely chopped

2 carrots, finely chopped

2 celery sticks, finely chopped

1 preserved lemon (see page 11), finely chopped

400-g tin plum tomatoes with their juice

150 ml fish stock or water

150 ml white wine or fino sherry

sea salt and freshly ground black pepper

leaves from a bunch of fresh mint, finely shredded

For the chermoula:

2–3 garlic cloves, chopped

1 red chilli, deseeded and chopped

1 teaspoon sea salt

a small bunch of fresh coriander

a pinch of saffron threads

1–2 teaspoons ground cumin

3–4 tablespoons olive oil

freshly squeezed juice of 1 lemon

Serves 4–6

First, make the chermoula. Using a mortar and pestle, pound the garlic and chilli with the salt to form a paste. Add the coriander leaves and pound to a coarse paste. Beat in the saffron threads and cumin and bind well with the olive oil and lemon juice (you can whizz all the ingredients together in an electric blender, if you prefer). Reserve 2 teaspoons of the mixture for cooking. Toss the fish chunks in the remaining chermoula, cover and leave to marinate in the refrigerator for 1–2 hours.

Heat the oil in a tagine or heavy-based casserole. Stir in the onion, carrots and celery and sauté until softened. Add the preserved lemon (reserving a little for sprinkling) with the reserved 2 teaspoons of chermoula and the tomatoes and stir in well. Cook gently for about 10 minutes to reduce the liquid, then add the stock and the wine or sherry. Bring the liquid to the boil, cover the tagine, reduce the heat and simmer for 10–15 minutes.

Toss the fish in the tagine, cover and cook gently for 6–8 minutes, until the fish is cooked through. Season to taste with salt and pepper, sprinkle with the reserved preserved lemon and the shredded mint leaves and serve immediately.

tagine of monkfish, potatoes, cherry tomatoes and black olives

For this lovely tagine, flavoured with garlic, chilli, cumin and coriander (a popular version of Morocco's favourite chermoula spice mix), you can used any meaty white fish. Serve it as a meal in itself with chunks of fresh, crusty bread to mop up the delicious juices, or with Plain, Buttery Couscous.

• •

1 quantity Chermoula (see page 12)

900 g monkfish tail, cut into chunks

12 small new potatoes

3 tablespoons olive oil plus a knob of butter

3–4 garlic cloves, thinly sliced

12–16 cherry tomatoes

2 green peppers, grilled until black, skinned and cut into strips

sea salt and freshly ground black pepper

12 black olives

1 lemon, cut into wedges, to serve

crusty bread or Plain, Buttery Couscous (see page 108), to serve

Serves 4-6

First, make the chermoula. Put the fish in a shallow dish and rub it with most of the chermoula (reserve a little for cooking). Cover and leave to marinate in the refrigerator for 1–2 hours.

Meanwhile, bring a saucepan of water to the boil and add the potatoes. Boil vigorously for about 8 minutes to soften them a little, then drain and refresh under cold running water. Peel and cut in half lengthways.

Heat 2 tablespoons of the olive oil with the butter in a tagine or heavy-based saucepan. Stir in the garlic and, when it begins to brown, add the tomatoes to soften them. Add the skinned peppers and the reserved chermoula, and season to taste with salt and pepper. Tip the mixture onto a plate.

Arrange the potatoes over the base of the tagine and spoon half of the tomato and pepper mixture over them. Place the chunks of marinated fish on top and spoon the rest of the tomato and pepper mixture over the fish. Tuck the olives in and around the fish and drizzle the remaining tablespoon of olive oil over the top. Pour in 125 ml of water, cover with a lid and steam for 15–20 minutes, until the fish is cooked through. Serve immediately with wedges of lemon.

saffron sea bass tagine with potatoes and peppers

This is one of the traditional oven-baked tagines, which are incredibly simple and satisfying. Versatile in nature, this dish can be altered to accommodate any selection of vegetables, such as leeks, courgettes, Swiss chard, broad beans and fennel.

◆ ◆

a pinch of saffron threads

150 ml warm water

900 g new potatoes, peeled and sliced

4 large tomatoes, sliced (reserve a few slices to top the fish)

4–6 garlic cloves, peeled and smashed

2 green peppers, deseeded and cut into long strips (reserve a few strips to top the fish)

4 tablespoons olive oil

freshly squeezed juice of 2 lemons

1 sea bass (roughly 1.25 kg), gutted and thoroughly cleaned

the rind of a small preserved lemon, or half a large one, cut into fine strips (see page 11)

2 tablespoons green olives, stoned and sliced

a small bunch of fresh coriander, finely chopped

sea salt and freshly ground black pepper

Serves 4–6

Preheat the oven to 180°C (350°F) Gas 4.

First prepare the saffron. Dry roast the threads in a small heavy-based frying pan for less than 1 minute, until they emit a faint aroma. Using a mortar and pestle, grind them to a powder and stir in the water until the saffron dissolves.

Line the base of an oven tagine, or an ovenproof dish, with a layer of potatoes, topped with a layer of sliced tomatoes. Scatter the garlic over the top, season with a little salt and pepper and arrange the peppers over the top. Pour half the prepared saffron, half the olive oil and half the lemon juice over the layers, cover and place it in the preheated oven for about 25 minutes, until the potatoes and peppers are tender but not soft.

Rub the sea bass with a little salt and place it on top of the peppers. Mark the topside of the fish with 2–3 gashes and pour the rest of the prepared saffron, olive oil and lemon juice over it. Arrange the reserved tomato and pepper slices over the top and scatter the preserved lemon and olives over and around the fish. Cover the tagine and return to the oven for another 25 minutes, until the fish is just cooked. Remove the lid and return the fish to the oven for a final 10 minutes. Scatter the coriander over the top and serve with crusty bread or Plain, Buttery Couscous.

oven-baked tagine of red mullet, tomatoes and lime

Baking whole fish in a tagine keeps the flesh deliciously moist. Obviously, you need to select fish that fits snugly into your tagine or ovenproof dish. The most popular fish for oven-baking in North Africa include red mullet, sardines, red snapper, grouper and sea bass. You could serve this dish with Plain, Buttery Couscous or a tangy salad.

* *

2 tablespoons olive oil

25 g butter

2–3 garlic cloves, thinly sliced

3–4 good-sized red mullet, gutted and cleaned

sea salt

2–3 large tomatoes, thinly sliced

1 lime, thinly sliced

To serve:

leaves from a small bunch of fresh flat leaf parsley, coarsely chopped

1 lime, cut into wedges

Serves 3–4

Preheat the oven to 180°C (350°F) Gas 4.

Heat the olive oil and butter in an oven tagine or ovenproof dish. Add the garlic and sauté, stirring, until it begins to brown. Put the fish in the tagine and cook it until the skin has browned and lightly buckled. (If you are using an ovenproof dish, brown the garlic and fish in a large frying pan first.)

Turn off the heat, sprinkle a little salt over the fish and tuck the slices of tomato and lime over and around them. Cover and cook in the preheated oven for about 15 minutes.

Uncover and bake for a further 5–10 minutes, until the fish is cooked and nicely browned on top (you could do this under the grill, if you prefer).

Sprinkle the parsley over the top and serve with wedges of lime to squeeze over the fish.

prawn tagine with saffron, ginger and fennel

Many shellfish tagines are not so much traditional as they are inspired by cultural influences, such as the prawn and mussel tagines of Tangier that resemble the cooking of Andalusia across the water. Serve this delicious tagine as a first or second course with chunks of crusty bread.

4–5 tablespoons olive oil

20 raw king prawns, with heads removed

2 onions, finely chopped

2 garlic cloves, finely chopped

25 g fresh ginger, peeled and finely chopped

a pinch of saffron threads

1–2 teaspoons smoked paprika

400-g tin tomatoes, drained of juice

leaves from a small bunch of fresh coriander, finely chopped

leaves from a small bunch of fresh flat leaf parsley, finely chopped

1 teaspoon sugar

4 fennel bulbs, trimmed and sliced thickly lengthways

sea salt and freshly ground black pepper

crusty bread, to serve

Serves 4

Heat 2–3 tablespoons of the olive oil in the base of a tagine or heavy-based casserole. Add the prawns and cook for 2–3 minutes, until they turn opaque. Using a slotted spoon, remove the prawns from the tagine and set aside. Keep the oil in the pan.

Stir the onion, garlic, ginger and saffron into the oil and sauté for 3–4 minutes, until they begin to colour. Add the paprika, tomatoes and half the herbs. Stir in the sugar and season with salt and pepper. Cook gently, partially covered, for about 10 minutes until the mixture thickens to form a sauce.

Meanwhile, steam the fennel for about 5 minutes, until it softens. Heat the remaining olive oil in a frying pan and add the steamed fennel. Cook gently on both sides for 4–5 minutes, until it turns golden. Sprinkle with salt and pepper.

Toss the cooked prawns in the tomato sauce, place the fennel on top, cover, and cook gently for 5 minutes. Sprinkle with the remaining coriander and parsley immediately before serving.

creamy shellfish tagine with fennel and harissa

In some coastal areas of Morocco, such as Casablanca and Tangier, restaurants offer shellfish tagines – a modern speciality, rather than a traditional one. Whether these dishes are the result of colonial French influence or simply devised for the tourists, they are certainly very tasty. They are best appreciated on their own, with chunks of crusty bread to mop up the creamy sauce.

◆ ◆

500 g fresh mussels in their shells, scrubbed clean and rinsed

500 g fresh prawns in their shells, thoroughly rinsed

freshly squeezed juice of 1 lemon

2 tablespoons olive oil

4–6 shallots, finely chopped

1 fennel bulb, chopped

1–2 teaspoons harissa paste (see page 12)

150 ml double cream

sea salt and freshly ground black pepper

leaves from a large bunch of fresh coriander, finely chopped

crusty bread, to serve

Serves 4–6

Put the mussels and prawns in a large saucepan with just enough water to cover them. Add the lemon juice, cover the pan and bring the liquid to the boil. Shake the pan and cook the shellfish for about 3 minutes, until the shells of the mussels have opened. Drain the shellfish, reserve the liquor, and discard any mussels that have not opened. Refresh the mussels and prawns under cold running water and shell most of them (you can, of course, leave them all in their shells if you prefer, as long as you are prepared for messy eating).

Heat the olive oil in a tagine or heavy-based casserole. Add the shallots and fennel and sauté, stirring, until soft. Stir in the harissa and pour in 300 ml of the reserved cooking liquor. Bring the liquid to the boil and continue to boil for 2–3 minutes, reduce the heat and stir in the cream. Simmer gently for about 5 minutes to let the flavours mingle, season to taste with salt and plenty of black pepper, and stir in the mussels and prawns. Toss in half the coriander, cover and cook gently for about 5 minutes. Sprinkle the remaining coriander over the top and serve immediately with crusty bread.

vegetable tagines

tagine of butternut squash, shallots, sultanas and almonds

Substantial enough for a main meal, served with Plain, Buttery Couscous and yoghurt, vegetable tagines also make good side dishes for grilled or roasted meats or other tagines. You can cook this recipe in the oven if you like, using the tagine base or an ovenproof dish.

• •

3 tablespoons olive oil plus a knob of butter

12 shallots, peeled and left whole

8 garlic cloves, lightly crushed

120 g sultanas

120 g blanched almonds

1–2 teaspoons harissa paste (see page 12)

2 tablespoons dark, runny honey

1 medium butternut squash, halved lengthways, peeled, deseeded and sliced

sea salt and freshly ground black pepper

leaves from a small bunch of fresh coriander, finely chopped

lemon wedges, to serve

Plain, Buttery Couscous (see page 108), to serve (optional)

Serves 3–4

Heat the oil and butter in a tagine or heavy-based casserole. Add the shallots and garlic and sauté, stirring, until they begin to colour. Add the sultanas and almonds and stir in the harissa and honey. Toss in the squash, making sure it is coated in the spicy oil. Pour in enough water to cover the base of the tagine and cover. Cook gently for 15–20 minutes, until the shallots and squash are tender but still quite firm.

Season to taste with salt and pepper, sprinkle the coriander leaves over the top and serve with wedges of lemon to squeeze over the dish and Plain, Buttery Couscous, if liked.

tagine of artichokes, potatoes, peas and saffron

You can make this hearty country dish with either fresh or frozen artichokes. If using fresh, you must first remove the outer leaves, then cut off the stems and scoop out the choke and hairy bits with a teaspoon. Rub the artichokes with lemon juice or place in a bowl of cold water with lemon juice to prevent discoloration.

• •

2–3 tablespoons olive oil

2 red onions, halved lengthways, cut in half crossways, and sliced with the grain

4 garlic cloves, crushed

2 teaspoons coriander seeds

1 teaspoon cumin seeds

2 teaspoons ground turmeric

1–2 teaspoons dried mint

8 medium waxy potatoes, peeled and quartered

350 ml vegetable or chicken stock

4 prepared artichokes, quartered

leaves from a small bunch of fresh coriander, chopped

225 g shelled fresh peas or frozen peas

½ preserved lemon (see page 11), finely shredded

sea salt and freshly ground black pepper

leaves from a small bunch of fresh mint, to serve

crusty bread or Plain, Buttery Couscous (see page 108), to serve

Serves 4–6

Heat the olive oil in a tagine or heavy-based casserole. Add the onion and sauté, stirring, until it begins to soften. Add the garlic, coriander and cumin seeds, ground turmeric and the dried mint. Toss in the potatoes, coating them in the spices. Pour in the stock and bring to the boil. Reduce the heat, cover and cook gently for about 10 minutes.

Toss in the artichokes and fresh coriander and cook for a further 5 minutes. Stir in the peas and preserved lemon, and season to taste with salt and pepper. Cook gently for 5–10 minutes, uncovered, until the artichokes are tender and the liquid has reduced.

Sprinkle with the fresh mint leaves and serve with crusty bread or Plain, Buttery Couscous.

tagine of yam, shallots, carrots and prunes

This syrupy, caramelized tagine is delicious served as a main dish,
with Plain, Buttery Couscous and a herby salad, or as a side dish to accompany
grilled or roasted meats. Sweet potatoes, butternut squash and pumpkin
can be used instead of yam, if you prefer.

• •

2–3 tablespoons olive oil plus
a knob of butter

40 g fresh ginger, peeled and finely
chopped or grated

1–2 cinnamon sticks or 1–2 teaspoons
ground cinnamon

16 small shallots, peeled and
left whole

700 g yam, peeled and cut into
bite-sized pieces

2 medium carrots, peeled and cut into
bite-sized pieces

175 g ready-to-eat stoned prunes

1 tablespoon dark, runny honey

425 ml vegetable or chicken stock

leaves from a small bunch of fresh
coriander, roughly chopped

a few fresh mint leaves, chopped

sea salt and freshly ground
black pepper

Plain, Buttery Couscous (see page
108), to serve (optional)

Serves 4–6

Heat the olive oil and butter in a tagine or heavy-based
casserole. Add the ginger and cinnamon sticks. Toss in
the shallots and when they begin to colour add the yam
and the carrots. Sauté for 2–3 minutes, stirring, then
add the prunes and the honey. Pour in the stock and
bring it to the boil. Reduce the heat, cover and cook
gently for about 25 minutes.

Uncover and stir in some of the coriander and mint.
Season to taste with salt and pepper and reduce
the liquid, if necessary, by cooking for a further
2–3 minutes uncovered. The vegetables should be
tender and slightly caramelized in a very syrupy sauce.
Sprinkle with the remaining coriander and mint and
serve immediately with Plain, Buttery Couscous,
if liked.

tagine of butter beans, cherry tomatoes and black olives

As butter beans are so meaty, this tagine makes a substantial main dish, but it is also excellent as an accompaniment to grilled or roasted meats and poultry. Bean dishes like this vary from region to region in Morocco, sometimes spiked with chillies or hot merguez, chorizo-style sausages.

* *

175 g dried butter beans, soaked overnight in plenty of water

2–3 tablespoons olive oil plus a knob of butter

4 garlic cloves, halved and crushed

2 red onions, halved lengthways, cut in half crossways, and sliced with the grain

1–2 red or green chillies, deseeded and thinly sliced

1–2 teaspoons coriander seeds, crushed

25 g fresh ginger, peeled and finely shredded or chopped

a pinch of saffron threads

16–20 cherry tomatoes

1–2 teaspoons sugar

1–2 teaspoons dried thyme

2–3 tablespoons black olives, stoned

freshly squeezed juice of 1 lemon

sea salt and freshly ground black pepper

leaves from a small bunch of flat leaf parsley, coarsely chopped

crusty bread and natural yoghurt, to serve (optional)

Serves 4–6

Drain and rinse the soaked beans. Put them in a deep saucepan with plenty of water and bring to the boil. Boil for about 5 minutes, then reduce the heat and simmer gently for about 1 hour, or until the beans are tender but not mushy. Drain and refresh under cold running water.

Heat the olive oil and butter in a tagine or heavy-based casserole. Add the garlic, onions and chillies and sauté, stirring, until they soften. Add the coriander seeds, ginger and saffron. Cover and cook gently for 4–5 minutes. Toss in the tomatoes with the sugar and thyme, cover with the lid again, and cook until the skin on the tomatoes begins to crinkle.

Toss in the beans and olives, pour over the lemon juice and season to taste with salt and pepper. Cover and cook gently for about 5 minutes, until the beans and olives are heated through. Sprinkle with the flat leaf parsley and serve with crusty bread and a dollop of thick, creamy natural yoghurt, if liked.

tagine of baby aubergines with coriander and mint

This vegetarian tagine is best made with baby aubergines, but you can also use slender, larger aubergines cut into quarters lengthways. As a main dish, it is delicious served with Plain, Buttery Couscous and a dollop of thick, creamy yoghurt; it can also be served as a side dish to accompany meat or poultry.

* *

1–2 tablespoons olive oil

1 tablespoon butter or ghee

1–2 red onions, halved lengthways and sliced with the grain

3–4 garlic cloves, crushed

1–2 red chillies, deseeded and sliced, or 2–3 dried red chillies, left whole

1–2 teaspoons coriander seeds, roasted and crushed

1–2 teaspoons cumin seeds, roasted and crushed

2 teaspoons sugar

16 baby aubergines, with stalks intact

2 x 400-g tins chopped tomatoes

sea salt and freshly ground black pepper

leaves from a bunch of fresh mint, roughly chopped

leaves from a bunch of fresh coriander, roughly chopped

Plain, Buttery Couscous (see page 108) and natural yoghurt, to serve (optional)

Serves 4

Heat the oil and butter in a tagine or heavy-based casserole. Add the onions and garlic and sauté, stirring, until they begin to colour. Add the chillies, the coriander and cumin seeds and the sugar. When the seeds give off a nutty aroma, toss in the whole baby aubergines, coating them in the onion and spices. Tip in the tomatoes, cover and cook gently for about 40 minutes, until the aubergines are beautifully tender.

Season to taste with salt and pepper and add half the mint and coriander leaves. Cover and simmer for a further 5–10 minutes. Sprinkle with the remaining mint and coriander leaves and serve hot with Plain, Buttery Couscous and a dollop of thick, creamy natural yoghurt, if liked.

spicy carrot and chickpea tagine with turmeric and coriander

This country-style dish is vegetarian, typical of regions where meat is regarded as a luxury by most families. Pulses of all kinds and, in particular, chickpeas, provide the nourishing content of these dishes. To avoid lengthy preparation and cooking, use tinned chickpeas. For simple accompaniments, offer natural yoghurt and bread.

• •

3–4 tablespoons olive oil

1 onion, finely chopped

3–4 garlic cloves, finely chopped

2 teaspoons ground turmeric

1–2 teaspoons cumin seeds

1 teaspoon ground cinnamon

½ teaspoon cayenne pepper

½ teaspoon ground black pepper

1 tablespoon dark, runny honey

3–4 medium carrots, sliced on the diagonal

2 x 400-g tins chickpeas, rinsed and drained

sea salt

1–2 tablespoons rosewater

leaves from a bunch of fresh coriander, finely chopped

lemon wedges, to serve

crusty bread and natural yoghurt, to serve (optional)

Serves 4

Heat the oil in a tagine or heavy-based casserole. Add the onion and garlic and sauté, stirring, until soft. Add the turmeric, cumin seeds, cinnamon, cayenne pepper, black pepper, honey and carrots. Pour in enough water to cover the base of the tagine and cover. Cook gently for about 10–15 minutes.

Toss in the chickpeas, check that there is still enough liquid at the base of the tagine, adding a little more water if necessary. Cover with the lid, and cook gently for 5–10 minutes until all the vegetables are tender.

Season with salt, sprinkle the rosewater and coriander leaves over the top and arrange the lemon wedges on the side. Serve with crusty bread and a dollop of thick, creamy natural yoghurt, if liked.

baked vegetable tagine with preserved lemon

This vegetable tagine can be served as a side dish or on its own with Plain, Buttery Couscous or flat bread to dip into it. Vegetable tagines vary with the seasons and can be prepared on the hob or in the oven. For the baked version, you need a traditional Berber tagine with a domed lid, rather than the steep conical one, or you can use an earthenware baking dish, covered with foil.

* *

2–3 tablespoons olive oil

*2 onions, halved and sliced
with the grain*

4 garlic cloves, chopped

*a thumb-sized piece of fresh ginger,
peeled and chopped*

1–2 red chillies, deseeded and chopped

1 teaspoon cumin seeds

1 teaspoon paprika

*3–4 good-sized potatoes, peeled
and thickly sliced*

*2 good-sized carrots, peeled
and thickly sliced*

8–10 broccoli florets

600 ml vegetable or chicken stock

225 g fresh or frozen peas

*1 preserved lemon (see page 11),
thickly sliced*

*leaves from a bunch of fresh
coriander, coarsely chopped*

*sea salt and freshly ground
black pepper*

4–6 large tomatoes, sliced

15 g butter

*crusty bread or Plain, Buttery
Couscous (see page 108), to serve*

Serves 4

Preheat the oven to 180°C (350°F) Gas 4.

Heat the oil in a tagine or heavy-based casserole. Add the onions and sauté until they begin to colour. Add the garlic, ginger and chillies and cook for 1–2 minutes. Stir in the cumin seeds and paprika then toss in the potatoes, carrots and broccoli. Pour in the stock, cover and place the tagine in the oven for about 20 minutes, until the potatoes, carrots and broccoli are tender but still firm and most of the liquid has reduced.

Season with salt and pepper. Toss in the peas, preserved lemon and half the coriander. Arrange the tomato slices, overlapping each other, on top and dab them with little bits of butter. Pop the tagine back into the oven, uncovered, to brown the top of the tomatoes.

Garnish with the remaining coriander and serve hot from the tagine with Plain, Buttery Couscous or crusty bread.

three pepper tagine with eggs

This is one of those dishes you'll find in Morocco at street stalls, bus stations and working men's cafes. Quick, easy and colourful, it is a great dish for lunch or a tasty snack, served with warmed flat breads.

• •

2 tablespoons olive oil or ghee

1 onion, halved lengthways and sliced

2–3 garlic cloves, chopped

1–2 teaspoons coriander seeds

1 teaspoon cumin seeds

3 peppers (green, red and yellow), deseeded and cut into slices

2 tablespoons green olives, stoned and finely sliced

sea salt and freshly ground black pepper

4–6 very fresh eggs

1 teaspoon paprika or dried red chilli flakes

leaves from a small bunch of flat leaf parsley, coarsely chopped

warmed flat breads, to serve

Serves 4–6

Heat the oil in the base of a tagine, flameproof baking dish or heavy-based frying pan. Add the onions, garlic, cumin and coriander seeds and sauté, stirring, until the onions begin to soften. Toss in the peppers and olives and sauté until they begin to colour. Season well with salt and pepper.

Using your spoon, push aside the peppers to form little pockets for the eggs. Crack the eggs in the pockets and cover for 4–5 minutes until the eggs are cooked. Scatter the paprika over the top and sprinkle with the parsley. Serve immediately from the tagine or pan, with warmed flat bread on the side.

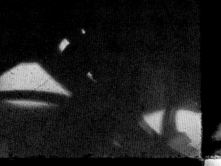

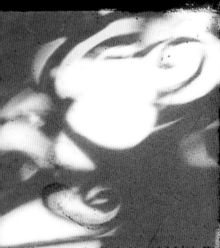

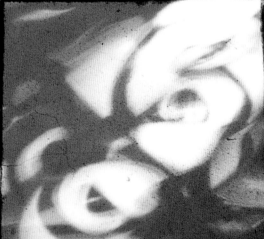

couscous
dishes

the art of making couscous

Couscous is Morocco's national dish. It is prepared throughout the country and is a traditional staple of the whole of the North African region, right down to Senegal and across to Chad. Further east in Egypt and parts of the Middle East, it is known as *moghrabiyyeh*, 'the dish of the North Africans'. Although referred to as a 'grain', couscous is not technically one; instead it could be more accurately described as Moroccan 'pasta' as it is made with semolina flour and water and then hand-rolled and dried even though it is prepared and served like rice.

Couscous is of fundamental value to Moroccan culture for dietary, religious and symbolic reasons, as Moroccans believe it is a food that brings God's blessing upon those who consume it. It is therefore prepared in every household on Muslim holy days and on Fridays, the Islamic day of rest, when it is

traditionally distributed to the poor as well. At festive and religious feasts, such as the traditional *diffas* to celebrate births and weddings, or the Berber *moussems*, a mound of couscous is served as the magnificent crown to end the meal. There is a Moroccan saying that 'each granule of couscous represents a good deed', so it is not surprising that thousands of granules are consumed in a day.

There are many different types of couscous in Morocco, some made with wheat flour, others with barley, maize or millet. In the rural areas, the village women still buy sacks of wheat, which they take to the local mill to be ground to semolina, and then laboriously prepare couscous every week by sprinkling the semolina flour with water and raking it with their fingers in a circular motion to form tiny balls. The balls are then rubbed against the side of the bowl using the palm of the hand and passed through a sieve to form a uniform size: *kesksou* is 2 mm in diameter; *seffa* or *mefuf* is ultra-fine at 1 mm in diameter and is mainly reserved for fillings and sweet dishes; and *mhammsa* is 3 mm in diameter. The tiny granules are then spread out to dry before use. In modern households in the cities, many cooks prefer to buy sacks of ready-prepared couscous which needs to be steamed several times before eating. Outside Morocco, the most commonly available packets of couscous have been taken one step further as they are already precooked and only require soaking in water to swell, before being fluffed up aerated using fingers and olive oil. The recipes in this book use this precooked version, which is available in supermarkets.

The preparation of couscous varies from region to region and is dependent on the type of granules, but the principal method involves placing the dried granules in a *ga'saa* – a wide, flat earthenware dish – and sprinkling them liberally with water. The moistened granules are then transferred to the metal *keskess*, a colander, and set snugly atop a *q'draa*, a large tin-lined, copper pot, which contains water or a stew of meat or vegetables. The utensils together are known in French as the two-tiered pot, the *couscoussière*, and this is the name that is used in international culinary circles. The steam between the *keskess* and the *q'draa* is sealed with a piece of cloth which is dipped in a mixture of flour and water. The couscous is then steamed, uncovered, until puffs of vapour emanate from the granules. The warm couscous is then returned to the *ga'saa* and mixed with more water before being returned to the

colander and steamed a second time until the granules become soft and plump. Finally it is flavoured with lashings of butter, olive oil or smen (see page 11), which is rubbed into the grains with the fingertips, and it is moistened with the broth from the stew. This preparation plays such an important role in the culinary life of most Moroccans that it determines a cook's ability – the granules should be light and airy, almost floating above the plate and heavenly to touch and taste.

To the majority of Moroccans a meal would be unthinkable without couscous. It is extremely versatile and is traditionally served as a course on its own, but it can also be served as an accompaniment to tagines or grilled and roasted meats. It can look truly spectacular, particularly when piled high in a cone-shaped mound for banquets and topped with stuffed pigeons, dates and almonds, or decorated with strips of colourful vegetables and topped with sweet onions and raisins tinged yellow with saffron and it is often accompanied by little side dishes, such as spicy chickpeas, marinated raisins and harissa paste (see page 12). Eating couscous in a traditional manner is an experience in itself and requires a little practice. It is a communal dish so, once the mound has been set on the ground, or on a low table, diners literally ram their right hands, palm upwards, into the grains to extract a handful and then, using the thumb and first two fingers, deftly roll the grains to form small tight balls that might incorporate some small pieces of meat or vegetables, and flip them into their mouths. It looks easy but, on first attempts, the sauce dribbles down your wrist and the granules spill all over the table!

plain, buttery couscous

Traditionally, plain, buttery couscous, piled high in a mound, is served as a dish on its own after a tagine or roasted meat. It is held in such high esteem that religious feasts and celebratory meals would be unthinkable with it. The par-boiled couscous available outside Morocco is extremely easy to prepare, making it a practical accompaniment for many dishes featured in this book.

• •

350 g couscous, rinsed and drained

½ teaspoon sea salt

400 ml warm water

2 tablespoons olive or sunflower oil

25 g butter, broken into little pieces

For the top:

15 g butter

2–3 tablespoons blanched, flaked almonds

Serves 4–6

Preheat the oven to 180°C (350°F) Gas 4.

Tip the couscous into an ovenproof dish. Stir the salt into the water and pour it over the couscous. Leave the couscous to absorb the water for about 10 minutes.

Using your fingers, rub the oil into the couscous grains to break up the lumps and aerate them. Scatter the butter over the surface and cover with a piece of foil or wet greaseproof paper. Put in the preheated oven for about 15 minutes, until the couscous is heated through.

Meanwhile, prepare the almonds. Melt the butter in a heavy-based frying pan set over medium heat, add the almonds and cook, stirring until they begin to turn golden. Remove from the pan and drain on kitchen paper.

Take the couscous out of the oven and fluff up the grains with a fork. Serve it from the dish or tip it onto a plate and pile it high in a mound, with the toasted almonds scattered over the top.

green couscous with a spring broth

This is a lovely spring or summer couscous dish as it is prepared with the young green vegetables in season, such as fresh broad beans and peas, artichokes, asparagus, rocket leaves, spring onions and baby courgettes.

◆ ◆

500 g couscous

½ teaspoon sea salt

600 ml warm water

1–2 tablespoons olive oil

15 g butter, broken into small pieces

1 litre vegetable or chicken stock

350 g fresh broad beans, shelled

200 g fresh or frozen peas

12 spring onions, trimmed and thickly sliced

6 baby courgettes, thickly sliced

4–6 globe artichoke hearts, cut into quarters

leaves from a bunch of fresh flat leaf parsley, finely chopped

leaves from a bunch of fresh coriander, finely chopped

leaves from a bunch of fresh mint, finely chopped

sea salt and freshly ground black pepper

Serves 4–6

Preheat the oven to 200°C (400°F) Gas 6.

Tip the couscous into an ovenproof dish. Stir the salt into the water and pour it over the couscous. Leave the couscous to absorb the water for about 10 minutes.

Using your fingers, rub the oil into the couscous grains to break up the lumps and aerate them. Scatter the butter over the surface and cover with a piece of foil or wet greaseproof paper. Put in the preheated oven for about 15 minutes, until the couscous is heated through.

Meanwhile, prepare the vegetable broth. Pour the stock into a heavy-based saucepan and bring it to the boil. Add the broad beans, peas, spring onions, courgettes and artichokes and cook for 5–10 minutes, until tender. Season the broth to taste with salt and pepper and stir in the herbs.

Remove the couscous from the oven and tip it onto a serving plate. Using a slotted spoon, lift the vegetables out of the broth and arrange them around, or over, the mound of couscous. Moisten with a little of the broth, then pour the rest into a jug and serve separately to pour over the couscous. Serve immediately.

lemon couscous with roasted vegetables

This is a modern recipe and ideal for vegetarians. For a variation, instead of roasting the vegetables, you could prepare vegetable kebabs on the barbecue and serve them with the couscous. Generally, aubergines, courgettes and peppers are roasted together but you can vary the vegetables, according to the season.

• •

8 baby aubergines, left whole

3–4 small courgettes, cut into
4 lengthways

2 red peppers, deseeded and cut into
4 lengthways

4 garlic cloves, peeled and cut into
4 lengthways

a thumb-sized piece of fresh ginger,
peeled and cut into thin sticks

100 ml olive oil

sea salt

leaves from a bunch of fresh
coriander, coarsely chopped

leaves from a bunch of fresh mint,
coarsely chopped

For the Lemon Couscous:

500 g couscous

½ teaspoon sea salt

600 ml warm water

1–2 tablespoons olive oil

1 preserved lemon (see page 11),
finely chopped

15 g butter, broken into small pieces

Serves 4

Preheat the oven to 200°C (400°F) Gas 6.

Put the vegetables, garlic and ginger in an ovenproof dish. Pour over the oil, sprinkle with salt and cook in the preheated oven for about 40 minutes, until the vegetables are tender and nicely browned.

To make the lemon couscous, tip the couscous into an ovenproof dish. Stir the salt into the water and pour it over the couscous. Leave it to absorb the water for about 10 minutes.

Using your fingers, rub the oil into the couscous grains to break up the lumps and aerate them. Toss in the preserved lemon, scatter the butter over the surface and cover with a piece of foil or wet greaseproof paper. Put the dish in the oven for about 15 minutes, until the couscous has heated through.

Tip the couscous onto a serving plate in a mound. Arrange the vegetables over and around it and spoon some of the roasting oil over the top. Sprinkle with the coriander and mint and serve immediately.

fish and shellfish k'dra with couscous

In the coastal regions, this is the king of fish dishes. Prepared in vast quantities for a family celebration, it combines the riches of the sea and the land in one big copper pot. Any firm-fleshed fish such as haddock, trout or sea bass will work here.

• •

2 tablespoons olive oil

2 teaspoons cumin seeds

2 teaspoons coriander seeds

2 teaspoons ground turmeric

1 tablespoon harissa paste
(see page 12)

leaves from a small bunch of
flat leaf parsley, finely chopped

2 litres fish stock or water

4–6 garlic cloves, finely sliced

2 x 400-g tins whole plum tomatoes,
drained of juice

2–3 carrots, cut into matchsticks

2–3 courgettes, cut into matchsticks

1 kg firm-fleshed fish fillets

450 g uncooked prawns, shelled
and deveined

450 g fresh mussels, cleaned

450 g scallops, shelled and cleaned

sea salt and freshly ground
black pepper

leaves from a small bunch of fresh
coriander, finely chopped

For the couscous:

350 g couscous, rinsed and drained

400 ml warm water

2 tablespoons olive or sunflower oil

25 g butter, broken into little pieces

Preheat the oven to 180°C (350°F) Gas 4.

Tip the couscous grains into an ovenproof dish. Stir ½ teaspoon salt into the water and pour it over the couscous. Set aside for about 20 minutes.

Meanwhile, heat the oil in a large copper pot, or very large heavy-based saucepan. Stir in the cumin and coriander seeds, turmeric and harissa paste. Add the parsley and pour in the fish stock. Bring the liquid to the boil, reduce the heat and simmer for 5 minutes. Add the garlic, tomatoes, carrots and courgettes and simmer for a further 10 minutes.

Using your fingers, rub the oil into the couscous grains to break up the lumps and aerate them. Scatter the butter over the top and cover with a piece of foil or wet greaseproof paper. Place in the oven for about 15 minutes to heat through.

Add the fish and shellfish to the simmering broth and cook for 5–10 minutes, until the fish is flaky, the prawns opaque, and the shells of the mussels have opened (discard any that remain closed). Season to taste with salt and pepper and stir in a little coriander.

Fluff up the couscous with a fork and pile it onto a large serving plate in a domed mound. Spoon the fish and shellfish around the couscous and drizzle with a little of the broth. Ladle the rest of the broth into individual bowls and serve immediately.

Serves 4–6

couscous tfaia with beef

This dish would traditionally be made in a *couscoussière* (see page 107) with the meat cooking in the bottom compartment creating the steam for the couscous above. However, the couscous can be prepared separately and the dish combined at the end. The tfaia is a sweet mixture of onions and sultanas that is spooned on top of the stew.

• •

750 g beef rump or chuck, cut into bite-sized pieces

1 onion, chopped

1 teaspoon ground coriander

1 teaspoon ground cumin

a pinch of saffron threads

500 g couscous

500 ml warm water

1–2 tablespoons olive oil

15 g butter, broken

For the tfaia:

1–2 tablespoons olive oil

25 g butter

4 onions, thinly sliced

1–2 teaspoons cinnamon

1 teaspoon ground ginger

1 teaspoon saffron threads, soaked in 2 tablespoons warm water

2 tablespoons runny honey

3 tablespoons sultanas, soaked in warm water for 15 minutes and drained

sea salt and freshly ground black pepper

Serves 4–6

Preheat the oven to 180°C (350°F) Gas 4.

Put the beef in the base of a tagine or heavy-based casserole with the onion, spices and saffron. Pour in just enough water to cover, then bring to the boil. Reduce the heat, cover and simmer for about 1 hour.

Meanwhile, tip the couscous into an ovenproof dish. Stir ½ teaspoon salt into the water and pour it over the couscous. Leave the couscous to absorb the water for about 10 minutes. Using your fingers, rub the oil into the couscous grains to break up the lumps and aerate them. Scatter the butter over the top and cover with a piece of foil or wet greaseproof paper. Put the dish in the preheated oven for about 15 minutes, until the couscous is heated through.

To prepare the tfaia, heat the oil and butter in a heavy-based saucepan. Add the onions and sauté for 1–2 minutes, until softened. Reduce the heat and add the spices, saffron water and honey and season to taste with salt and pepper. Cover and cook gently for 15–20 minutes. Stir in the sultanas and cook, uncovered, for a further 10 minutes.

Tip the couscous onto a serving dish and create a well in the centre. Using a slotted spoon, transfer the meat into the well and top with the tfaia. Strain the cooking liquid from the meat and serve it separately as a sauce.

salads and vegetable side dishes

country salad with peppers and chillies

Fresh country salads vary according to the season but generally they are crunchy and tangy, and often packed with fresh herbs to cleanse the palate. A salad may be offered at the start of the meal to whet the appetite, or as an accompaniment to the heavier, syrupy tagines to cut the sweetness.

2 red onions, finely chopped

1 red pepper, deseeded and chopped

1 green pepper, deseeded and chopped

2 green chillies, deseeded and chopped

2 celery sticks, chopped

2 garlic cloves, chopped

leaves from a large bunch each of fresh mint and flat leaf parsley, chopped

2 tablespoons olive oil

freshly squeezed juice of ½ a lemon

sea salt and freshly ground black pepper

Serves 4

In a bowl, mix together the chopped onions, peppers, chillies, celery, garlic, mint and parsley. Add the olive oil and lemon juice and season to taste with salt and pepper. Toss the salad thoroughly and serve immediately.

preserved lemon and tomato salad with capers

There are a variety of tomato-based salads that come under the banner *salade marocaine*, especially in the tourist areas. This particular recipe is a great favourite. Tart, fruity, crunchy and refreshing, it appears in various versions throughout Morocco.

5–6 large tomatoes, skinned, deseeded and cut into thick strips

1 red onion, cut in half lengthways, then in half crossways, and sliced with the grain

rind of 1 preserved lemon, cut into thin strips (see page 11)

2–3 tablespoons olive oil

freshly squeezed juice of ½ lemon

1–2 tablespoons capers, rinsed and drained

leaves from a small bunch each of fresh flat leaf parsley, coriander and mint, finely chopped

1 teaspoon paprika

sea salt and freshly ground black pepper

Serves 4–6

Put the tomatoes, onions and preserved lemon in a bowl. Add the olive oil and lemon juice and toss well. Season to taste with salt and pepper and set aside until ready to serve.

Just before serving, toss in the capers and herbs and scatter the paprika over the top.

See photograph on page 123.

spicy aubergine and tomato salad

This classic spicy aubergine and tomato salad, which can be written as *zahlouk* or *zaalouk*, is delicious served on its own with chunks of bread, or as part of a spread. It can be made with olive oil or argan oil, which is pressed from the nut inside the fruit of the argan tree indigenous to the Souss region of Morocco.

* *

2 large aubergines

4 large tomatoes

100 ml olive or argan oil

2–3 garlic cloves, crushed

1 teaspoon harissa paste (see page 12)

leaves from a small bunch each of fresh flat leaf parsley and coriander, finely chopped

freshly squeezed juice of 1 lemon

sea salt and freshly ground black pepper

1 teaspoon cumin seeds, roasted and ground

crusty bread, to serve

Serves 4

Preheat the oven to 200°C (400°F) Gas 6.

Put the aubergines on a baking tray and bake them in the preheated oven for about 30 minutes, until soft when you press them with a finger. Put the tomatoes in an ovenproof dish, pour over half the olive oil, and pop them in the oven to cook with the aubergines.

Remove the aubergines and tomatoes from the oven and leave until cool enough to handle. Using a sharp knife, cut the aubergines in half, scoop out the warm flesh and chop it to a pulp. Skin the tomatoes, cut them in half, scoop out the seeds and chop the flesh to a pulp.

Heat the rest of the oil in a heavy-based pan, add the garlic and fry until it begins to colour, stirring constantly. Add the tomatoes and harissa and cook over a medium heat for 5–8 minutes, until thick and pulpy. Add the aubergines, parsley and coriander. Stir in the lemon juice and season to taste with salt and pepper. Tip into a serving bowl and serve warm or at room temperature with a dusting of roasted cumin and chunks of crusty bread.

roasted courgette and apple salad with oranges

The courgette is a popular summer vegetable in Morocco and, as it marries well with fresh herbs and garlic, it appears frequently in salads and dips as well as in vegetable and meat tagines. Served as a starter or as an accompaniment to a meat and poultry main dish, this salad is delightfully refreshing.

* *

2 medium courgettes, trimmed, cut in half crossways and sliced lengthways

1 green apple, cored, cut in half lengthways and sliced crossways

3 tablespoons olive oil

freshly squeezed juice of 1 lemon

1 tablespoon runny honey

2 sweet oranges, peeled with pith removed

rind of ½ preserved lemon, finely shredded (see page 11)

leaves from a small bunch of fresh mint, shredded

sea salt

Serves 4–6

Preheat the oven to 200°C (400°F) Gas 6.

Put the sliced courgette and apple in an ovenproof dish and spoon over the oil. Cook in the preheated oven for about 20 minutes. Remove from the oven and pour over the lemon juice and honey. Return them to the oven for a further 10 minutes, until they have softened and are slightly golden in colour. Leave them to cool in the dish.

Prepare the oranges on a plate to catch the juice. Slice them thinly into neat circles, remove any pips and arrange them on a serving dish. Spoon the roasted courgette and apple on top of the oranges. Stir the orange juice that you have caught on the plate into the roasting juices in the baking dish and season with a little salt. Drizzle the juice over the salad and scatter the preserved lemon and mint over the top. Serve chilled or at room temperature.

chickpea salad with onions and paprika

Chickpeas, beans and lentils are consumed daily in rural Morocco, particularly in areas where meat is scarce or expensive. They are cooked in stews, added to couscous, and find their way into salads. This dish is particularly good served warm and is often topped with crumbled goats' cheese from the village.

• •

225 g dried chickpeas, soaked in plenty of cold water overnight

1 red onion, cut in half lengthways, then in half crossways, and sliced with the grain

4 garlic cloves, finely chopped

1 teaspoon ground cumin

1–2 teaspoons paprika

3 tablespoons olive oil

freshly squeezed juice of 1 lemon

leaves from a small bunch each of fresh flat leaf parsley and coriander, coarsely chopped

125 g firm goats' cheese or feta, crumbled (optional)

sea salt and freshly ground black pepper

crusty bread, to serve

Serves 4

Drain the chickpeas and put them in a deep saucepan. Cover with water and bring to the boil. Reduce the heat and simmer for about 45 minutes, until the chickpeas are tender but not mushy. Drain the chickpeas and remove any loose skins – you can rub them in a clean tea towel, or between your fingers, to remove them.

Tip the warm chickpeas into a bowl. Add the onion, garlic, cumin and paprika and toss in the olive oil and lemon juice while the chickpeas are still warm, making sure they are all well coated. Season with salt and pepper to taste and toss in most of the parsley and coriander. Crumble over the goats' cheese, if using, and sprinkle with the rest of the herbs. Serve while still warm with chunks of crusty bread.

sautéed spinach with orange and almonds

This dish is generally made with spinach or mallow, which grows wild in the countryside and is picked for vegetable dishes and soup. Quite often you will come across makeshift stalls selling bunches of mallow by the dusty roadside.

500 g fresh spinach leaves, thoroughly rinsed and drained

2–3 tablespoons olive oil plus a knob of butter

1 onion, roughly chopped

2 garlic cloves, finely chopped

freshly squeezed juice and rind of 1 orange

2 tablespoons flaked almonds, toasted

sea salt and freshly ground black pepper

Serves 2–4

Put the spinach in a steamer and cook for 8–10 minutes, until soft. Tip the cooked spinach onto a wooden board and chop to a pulp. Set aside.

Heat the oil and butter in a heavy-based saucepan. Stir in the onion and garlic and cook until they begin to colour. Add the spinach and mix until thoroughly combined. Add the orange juice and rind and season to taste with salt and pepper. Tip the spinach into a serving dish and garnish with the toasted almonds.

braised fennel and courgette with aniseed

Braised vegetables, such as courgettes and artichokes, are often combined with fruit or spices and served as accompaniment to tagines or roasted meats. This recipe from Casablanca is light and aromatic rather than spicy and complements the fish tagines in this book.

3–4 tablespoons olive oil

2 fennel bulbs, trimmed and chopped

2 courgettes, trimmed and cut into cubes

1 tablespoon butter

2 teaspoons aniseeds

½ preserved lemon, very thinly sliced (see page 11)

sea salt and freshly ground black pepper

Serves 4

Heat the oil in a heavy-based saucepan and stir in the fennel. Cover with a lid and cook gently for 10–15 minutes. Stir in the courgettes and cook for a further 5 minutes, until they begin to soften.

Add the butter and the aniseeds and toss thoroughly. Season to taste with salt and pepper, sprinkle with the preserved lemon and serve immediately.

honey-glazed pumpkin with spices

Root vegetables and members of the squash family, such as sweet potatoes, turnips, butternut and pumpkins, are often cooked with honey and spices as their sweet flesh remains succulent and marries well with the flavours. Generally, these side dishes are served with grilled or roasted meats.

* *

700 g pumpkin flesh, with skin and seeds removed

50 g butter

2–3 tablespoons runny honey

2 cinnamon sticks

3–4 cloves

1 teaspoon ground ginger

½ teaspoon cayenne pepper

a small bunch of fresh coriander, finely chopped

sea salt and freshly ground black pepper

Serves 4

Preheat the oven to 180°C (350°F) Gas 4.

Put the pumpkin in a steamer and cook for about 10 minutes, until the flesh is tender but still firm. Tip the steamed flesh into an ovenproof dish.

Melt the butter in a saucepan and stir in the honey. Add the cinnamon sticks, cloves, ground ginger and cayenne and season to taste with salt and pepper. Pour the mixture over the pumpkin then bake in the preheated oven for 15–20 minutes.

Tip the glazed pumpkin onto a serving plate, remove the cinnamon and cloves, then sprinkle with the coriander. Serve warm as a side dish to roasted or grilled chicken or meat.

Moroccan ratatouille with dates

Similar to a French ratatouille, this delicious dish is spiked with a touch of *ras-el-hanout* and sweetened with succulent dates. Serve it with bread or Plain, Buttery Couscous or as an accompaniment to a tagine, grilled meats or fish.

* *

4–5 tablespoons olive oil

1 onion, halved lengthways and sliced crossways

2 garlic cloves, chopped

1 red pepper, deseeded and halved lengthways and sliced crossways

1 aubergine, halved lengthways and sliced crossways

2 courgettes, sliced

225 g ready-to-eat stoned dates, halved lengthways

2 x 400-g tins chopped tomatoes

1–2 teaspoons sugar

2 teaspoons ras-el-hanout (see page 15)

leaves from a small bunch of fresh flat leaf parsley, coarsely chopped

sea salt and freshly ground black pepper

Plain, Buttery Couscous (see page 108), to serve (optional)

Serves 4–6

Heat the oil in a tagine or a heavy-based casserole. Add the onion and garlic and cook for 2–3 minutes until they begin to soften.

Add the pepper, aubergine and courgettes and cook for a further 3–4 minutes. Add the dates, tomatoes, sugar and ras-el-hanout and mix thoroughly. Cover and cook for about 40 minutes, until the vegetables are tender.

Season to taste with salt and pepper and sprinkle the chopped parsley over the top. Serve hot with Plain, Buttery Couscous or as a vegetable accompaniment to a tagine, grilled meats or fish.

melon and mint salad with orange flower water

This refreshing salad is an ideal accompaniment to spicy tagines. It is also served as a palate cleanser between the richly flavoured tagine and the ensuing course of a plain or lightly flavoured couscous.

1 ripe honeydew or galia melon, deseeded and cut into bite-sized chunks

leaves from a bunch of fresh mint, finely shredded (reserve a few leaves to garnish)

2 tablespoons orange flower water

1 tablespoon sugar or clear honey (optional)

Serves 4

In a bowl, toss the melon chunks with the mint and orange flower water, and sugar or honey, if using. Cover and chill in the refrigerator for 1–2 hours. Sprinkle with a few mint leaves and serve.

See photograph on page 139.

orange salad with red onion and black olives

Juicy salads made with citrus fruits, such as oranges and grapefruits, are popular accompaniments to the spicier, and sometimes fiery, tagines. Colourful and refreshing, this salad is also delicious served with grilled and roasted meats.

3 fresh oranges, peeled with a knife to remove the pith, and thinly sliced

1 red onion, thinly sliced into rings

12 black olives, stoned

2–3 tablespoons olive oil

freshly squeezed juice of 1 lime

sea salt

1 teaspoon cumin seeds, roasted

½ teaspoon smoked paprika

leaves from a small bunch of fresh coriander, coarsely chopped

Serves 4

Arrange the orange slices on a serving dish or in a shallow bowl and place the onion slices and olives on top.

In a small bowl, whisk together the olive oil and lime juice and add salt to taste. Pour the dressing over the oranges. Sprinkle the cumin seeds, paprika and coriander leaves over the top and serve.

INDEX